ANIMALS

Meerkats

by Robyn Weaver

Consultant:
Pam Wallberg
Consultant to *The Lion King* movie
Director, Fellow Earthlings–
A facility for the care of meerkats

Bridgestone Books
an imprint of Capstone Press
Mankato, Minnesota

Bridgestone Books are published by Capstone Press
818 North Willow Street, Mankato, Minnesota 56001
http://www.capstone-press.com

Library of Congress Cataloging-in-Publication Data
Weaver, Robyn
    Meerkats/by Robyn Weaver.
        p. cm.—(Animals)
    Includes bibliographical references and index.
    Summary: Introduces the meerkat's physical characteristics, habits, food, and relationship
to humans.
        ISBN 0-7368-0066-2
        1. Meerkat—Juvenile literature. [1. Meerkat.] I. Title. II. Series: Animals (Mankato, Minn.)
QL737.C235W435   1999
599.74—dc21

                                                                            98-17332
                                                                                CIP
                                                                                 AC

Editorial credits
Matt Doeden, editor; Timothy Halldin, cover designer; Sheri Gosewisch, photo researcher

Photo credits
Bruce Coleman/Bruce Coleman Inc., 4, 12
Frank S. Balthis, 20
G. C. Kelley, 10
Natural Exposures/Daniel J. Cox, 8, 14, 18
Phillip Roullard, 6
Photri-Microstock, cover
Visuals Unlimited/Gil Lopez-Espina, 16

Table of Contents

Tail

Underside

Claws

Nose

Fast Facts

Family: Meerkats belong to the mongoose family. A family is a group of animals with similar features.

Range: Meerkats live in southern Africa.

Habitat: Meerkats live on hot, dry land. Many live in the Kalahari Desert.

Food: Meerkats eat insects, small lizards, and small snakes. They also eat bird eggs and some plants.

Mating: Meerkats mate at any time during the year. Female meerkats give birth about 11 weeks after mating.

Young: Young meerkats are called kits. Kits are fully grown at about six months old.

Meerkats

Meerkats are members of the mongoose family. A family is a group of animals with similar features.

The word meerkat means mongoose in Afrikaans. Afrikaans is a language in South Africa. The scientific name for meerkats is *suricata suricatta*. Some African people call meerkats suricates (SUR-uh-kates).

Meerkats are mammals. Mammals are warm-blooded animals with backbones. The body heat of warm-blooded animals stays about the same. Their body heat does not change with the weather.

Meerkats spend much of their time lying in the sun. They lie on their backs. Meerkats may do this alone or in groups.

Meerkats spend much of their time lying in the sun.

Appearance

Meerkats have gray or brown fur. They have long, black noses and black fur around their eyes. Meerkats have white fur on their undersides. They have brown stripes on their backs.

Meerkats' bodies are thin. They grow up to 12 inches (30 centimeters) tall. Meerkats can weigh up to two pounds (one kilogram).

Meerkats have long tails with black tips. Their tails grow to be about eight inches (20 centimeters) long.

Meerkats have four toes on each paw. Each toe has a curved, black claw. Meerkats use their claws to dig burrows. A burrow is a hole in the ground where an animal lives.

Meerkats have brown stripes on their backs.

Homes

Meerkats live in southern Africa. The soil in southern Africa is hard and rocky. Many meerkats live in southern Africa's Kalahari Desert. The desert is often hot and dry.

Meerkats live in large groups called colonies. Usually about 30 meerkats live together in one colony. The meerkats in a colony share a burrow.

Meerkat burrows have long tunnels with many openings. Meerkats enter their burrows through holes in the ground. The holes are four to five inches (10 to 13 centimeters) wide.

Meerkats often use burrows that other animals once used. Some meerkats dig new burrows. They line their burrows with grass and dried plants.

Meerkats live in burrows.

Mating and Young

Meerkats can mate when they are about one year old. Mate means to join together to produce young. Meerkats can mate at any time during the year.

Females give birth about 11 weeks after they mate. They give birth inside burrows. Females usually have from two to four young meerkats called kits.

Newborn kits weigh about two ounces (57 grams). Their eyes are closed when they are born. Their eyes stay closed for about two weeks. Newborn kits have very little fur. They depend on adult meerkats to care for them. All the adult meerkats in a colony care for kits.

Kits stay in their burrows until about three weeks after birth. They are fully grown at about six months old.

Young meerkats depend on adult meerkats to care for them.

Colonies

Meerkats live and work together in colonies. Meerkats depend on each other for food and safety.

Each meerkat in a colony has a job. Some meerkats guard the colony from predators. A predator is an animal that hunts and eats other animals.

Meerkat guards stand on their back legs. They stretch their bodies so they can see far away. They make loud calls if they see a predator. They have a different call for each kind of predator.

Other meerkats care for kits. People call these meerkats baby-sitters. Baby-sitters care for a mother's kits when she hunts.

Some meerkats are baby-sitters.

Food

Meerkats eat mainly insects. They eat grasshoppers, beetles, and spiders. They also hunt mice, small lizards, and small snakes. Meerkats sometimes eat bird eggs.

Meerkats are able to eat some animals that would poison other predators. They are not harmed by some kinds of venom. Meerkats can eat venomous scorpions and some kinds of venomous snakes.

Meerkats also eat some plants. They eat roots and tubers. Tubers are the thick underground stems of some plants.

Meerkats hunt in groups. They hunt in different places each day. They do this to keep food supplies from running out.

Meerkats are able to eat some animals that would poison other predators.

Enemies

Eagles and jackals hunt meerkats that have left their burrows. They usually try to find meerkats that are alone.

Ratels also hunt meerkats. Ratels are a kind of weasel. Ratels dig into meerkat burrows. Meerkats escape through tunnel openings when ratels enter the burrows.

Meerkats avoid predators. Meerkat guards watch for predators. They make noises to warn other meerkats of danger. This gives the meerkats time to escape.

Meerkats form groups if they cannot escape from a predator. They hiss at the predator. They may jump at it. This scares some predators away. Meerkats may attack predators that come too close.

Meerkats form groups if they cannot escape from a predator.

Meerkats and People

Meerkats and people rarely live near one another. Meerkats live in dry areas where few people want to live.

Some people in southern Africa keep meerkats as outdoor pets. Meerkats do not show a strong fear of people. They eat many pests such as mice.

But meerkats do not make good pets. They may bite people if they sense danger. Meerkats also can destroy property. They dig through floors and walls.

Meerkats are like people in some ways. They work together. They each have different jobs within their groups. And they need the company of others of their kind.

Meerkats do not show a strong fear of people.

Hands on: Build Tunnels

Meerkats live in burrows. The burrows have many tunnels. You can build a small burrow with tunnels.

What You Need

1 flat piece of cardboard
1 spoon
2 cups (.5 liters) flour

1 large mixing bowl
1 cup (.25 liters) salt
1 cup (.25 liters) water

What You Do

1. Ask an adult to help you with this activity.
2. Mix the flour and salt in the mixing bowl. Slowly add water to the mix. Stir the mix with the spoon. Add water until the mix is a soft paste.
3. Place the paste on the cardboard. Use your finger to dig tunnels. You can make the tunnels any size you like. Make many openings. Imagine how a meerkat might dig tunnels.

Words to Know

burrow (BUR-oh)—a hole in the ground where an animal lives

mammal (MAM-uhl)—a warm-blooded animal with a backbone

predator (PRED-uh-tur)—an animal that hunts and eats other animals

tuber (TOO-bur)—the thick underground stem of a plant

venom (VEN-uhm)—poisonous liquid produced by some animals

Read More

Chinery, Michael. *Desert Animals*. New York: Random House, 1992.

Tesar, Jenny E. *What on Earth Is a Meerkat?* Woodbridge, Conn.: Blackbirch Press, 1994.

Useful Addresses

Fellow Earthlings
13 La Paz Lane
Palm Desert, CA 92260

Fort Worth Zoo
1989 Colonial Parkway
Fort Worth, TX 76110

Internet Sites

Meerkat
http://www.pbs.org/kratts/world/africa/meerkat/
index.html

The Meerkats at Fellow Earthlings
http://www.meerkats.com

Index